Copyright © The Archon Press 1979

Originated and produced by
The Archon Press Ltd
70, Old Compton Street
London W1V 5PA

First published in
Great Britain 1979 by
Hamish Hamilton Children's Books Ltd
Garden House, 57-59 Long Acre
London WC2E 9JL

Printed in Great Britain by
W S Cowell Ltd
Butter Market, Ipswich

ISBN 0 241 10252 9

Certain illustrations originally published in
The Closer Look Series

Apes

Consultant editor
Henry Pluckrose

Illustrated by
Richard Orr

small
WORLD

Hamish Hamilton · London

Humans, apes and monkeys
belong to the same order
of animals, a group
called the primates.

Monkey

Early man

Gorilla

People, monkeys and apes came from
a common ancestor which lived
millions of years ago.
This is why they look so alike today.
Apes and people differ from monkeys.
Apes and people have no tails,
longer arms, and more developed brains.
The apes are gorillas, orang-utans,
chimpanzees and gibbons.

Gibbon

Chimpanzee

Orang-utan

Gibbons are the smallest of the apes, the
lightest in weight, and the swiftest.
They have a special way of moving
through the trees.
They swing from hand to hand through
the highest branches.
Gibbons live in the tall trees of the rain
forests of South-East Asia.

9

A gibbon's feet can
grip like our hands.
Gibbons can run along
branches like
tight-rope walkers.
Their outstretched arms
help them to balance.

Gorillas are the largest of the Great Apes.
A fully-grown male gorilla standing
upright may be over 6 feet tall.
A male gorilla is fully mature at 12 years old.

Here is a family of
gorillas.

The Great Apes—the chimpanzees, gorillas and orang-utans—are all larger than the gibbons.
Gorillas and chimpanzees live in Africa. The orang-utan comes from the islands of Borneo and Sumatra in South-East Asia. The Great Apes look almost human—especially the chimpanzees.

Chimpanzee

You can see orang-utans in zoos today, but they are very rare in the wild.

This family of orang-utans consist of
a father, mother, and a baby.
Male orang-utans have pouches of skin
under their chins and in their cheeks.
In the Malay language, their name means
old man of the woods.
They do look rather like thoughtful old men
with their wrinkled faces and thin hair.

Today orang-utans
are found on the
islands of Borneo
and Sumatra.
Once they lived on
the mainland of
Asia, but there they
have been destroyed
by hunters.

Orang-utans live very quietly in the wild.
Like gibbons, they live in
tropical rain forests.
Unlike gibbons, however, orang-utans
are heavy and move slowly and carefully.

Orang-utans let go with
one foot at a time, always
holding the branches
with the other three.

Baby orang-utans look very appealing and
unfortunately are prized by animal collectors.
Hunters capture them by killing the mother
and stealing the baby, which will cling to
her even though she is dead.

When gorillas were first discovered
in the central African forests
in the last century, people thought
they were terrifying animals.
In fact, gorillas are very shy animals
which live together in family groups.
The head of the family is the senior
male gorilla called a silverback.

Because they are so
big, gorillas need to
eat a great deal.
They spend most of their
time gathering the
plants they feed on.

18

Gorillas use their
knuckles as well as
their feet to walk.

In spite of his fierce appearance, a fully-
grown male gorilla is really quite gentle.
He sometimes performs a fierce-looking dance—
hooting, chewing up branches, beating his
chest and stamping—but this is mostly show.
Gorillas can stand upright, but they usually
walk on all fours.

There are two types of gorilla.
The lowland gorilla lives in the West African
forests and the mountain gorilla lives on
the central African mountain slopes of
Zaire and Uganda.
This group of mountain gorillas is moving
through the bushes at the edge of the forest
in search of food.
The babies are clinging on to the backs
of their mothers.

Because they live in
a colder climate,
mountain gorillas
have thicker hair on
their bodies than
lowland gorillas.

Chimpanzees are the apes most people
know best.
They come from West and Central Africa
where they live in the rain forests and
in the trees at the edges of grassy plains.
They eat mostly fruit and vegetables, and
when these are scarce they will eat animals.
They usually live in groups which are
lead by a few males.

When chimpanzees
find a good source
of food they scream
and drum on their
chests because
they are so excited.

Chimpanzees are friendly, sociable animals
and very noisy.
Female chimpanzees are quieter than males.
Babies stay with their mothers until they
are at least six years old.
Very young babies cling to their mothers' fur.
Chimpanzees often hold hands and groom
each other.

Older babies ride on
their mothers' backs
on journeys.

Chimps
grooming

Of all animals, apes are the most intelligent.
The chimpanzees are probably the cleverest.
They can solve simple problems
and are quick to imitate and learn.
But they cannot keep their minds on
anything for very long.

This chimpanzee has
learned to use a weapon.
He is throwing stones at
baboons to drive them away.

These chimpanzees are doing something we might
think of as very human—using tools.
They are poking grass stalks into a termite nest.
The termites cling to the stalks.
The chimps pull the stalks out and
eat the termites.

Today many people are studying apes both in captivity and in their natural surroundings.
There is a lot to learn about these highly intelligent animals, our closest relatives in the animal world.

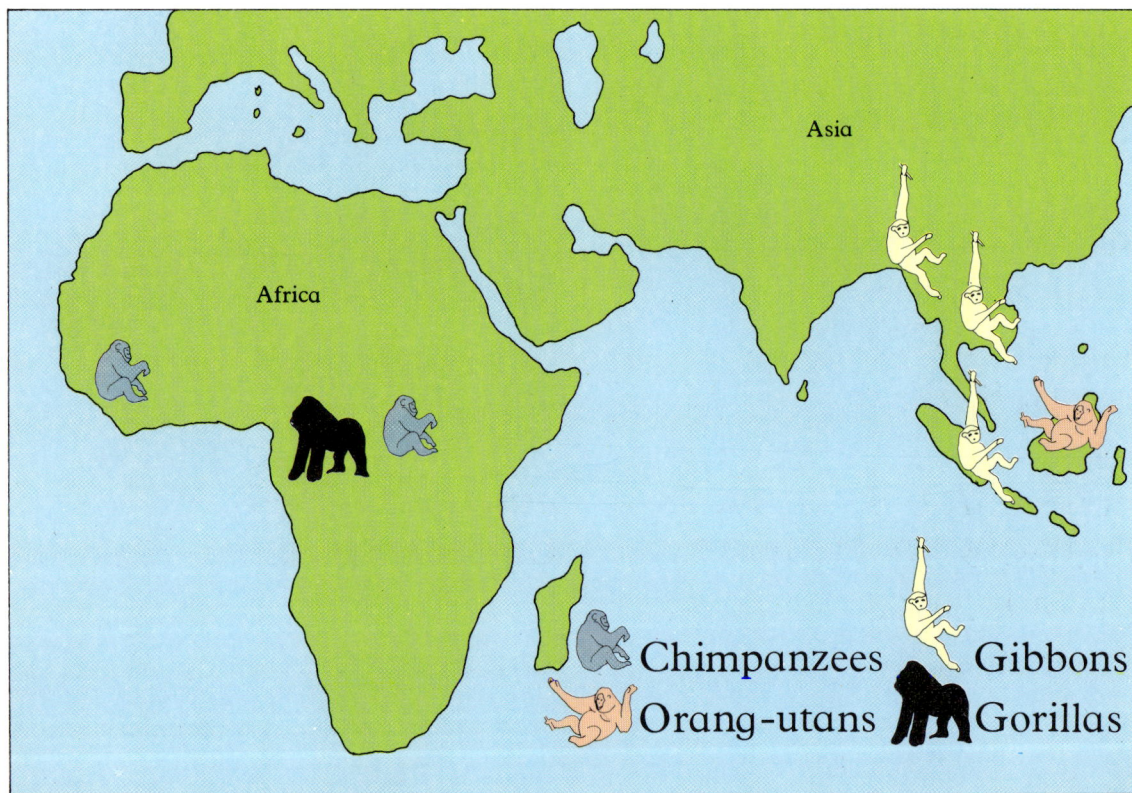

Asia

Africa

Chimpanzees   Gibbons
Orang-utans   Gorillas

Index